SOPHIA BLACKWELL

THE
OTHER
WOMAN

To Liz,

So lovely to meet you
in Archway!
Hope you enjoy.
All the best,
Sophia
xx

Burning Eye

BurningEyeBooks
Never Knowingly
Mainstream

Front cover shows Sophia and Heleana Blackwell
Photo © Krystyna FitzGerald-Morris

This edition published by Burning Eye Books 2018

www.burningeye.co.uk

@burningeyebooks

Burning Eye Books
15 West Hill, Portishead, BS20 6LG

ISBN 978-1-911570-52-3

SOPHIA BLACKWELL

THE
OTHER
WOMAN

To my family –
you know who you are.

CONTENTS

MIGRATIONS

I lost it in the tenth arrondissement
one rainy day when you refused to see –
or look up from your phone or back at me –
across the street, your longed-for restaurant,
the one place in Paris that cooked like Hoxton.
It seems our answer to thickening borders
and passport-glaring guards with armoured shoulders
is to make the world our own private London,
weigh up the charms of Spain and San Francisco
in rooftop bars. You boot up your computer,
seeking solutions, troubleshooting risks.
Truth is, each marriage has its own future,
and its own laws. A thin certificate
renders skin and gender a non-issue,

for us, for now. Our anthem is your breastbone
against my ear. Our histories twist with anger
but we know you can't make a meal of hunger,
and all our ancestors' turbulent crossings
have come to rest in us. Coins sewn in hems,
your sepia mother in tan leather gloves,
all chapters in a book that ends with love,
our friends' olive-skinned kids honouring them
at our table. The *Windrush* in you, the golden door
in me, it's all there. Let the wanderers come
from war to the ports, staggering up the shore
to find, like we did, London, Madrid, Rome –
me, in the middle, tugging your coat once more,
asking you if we're not already home.

BRIGHTON

Darling, I've got a plan. Let's go to Brighton.
We need some girl-time in the sea-sharp air,
chip fat and rain like perfume in our hair.
You've been not wearing colours for too long.

Let's set the clocks rattling back like wheels
out of Victoria. Let's light up Vogues
like wide-eyed students with new-minted loans
we think we won't pay back. Let's go to Brighton

and dance on bars, a pair of lairy aunties
wearing earrings you could fit a fist through,
latex and glitter, and laugh like we used to.
Let's chicken out of getting tattoos.

Let's sleep off hangovers in the faded roses
of B&Bs, hit the pleasure domes,
buy pink pails for gathering up stones,
sit half-cut in the dark, hear the sea groan

in front of us, its old unending blues
rolling over emails, traffic, Tubes,
husbands, lovers, everything we do
that gets between us being me and you.

VIXEN

It's like nothing on earth, my mother says
at breakfast, trying to describe the crying
of foxes fucking in the London night.
She pours her tea. *I thought someone was dying.*
I wonder what a Londoner would say.
I tell her you get used to it. I'm lying.

When I first heard it I thought the same thing
through a nightmare that grew new layers
with each scream. I stood at the window,
mocked by noise, sick with adrenaline,
seeing nothing but pale shuttered houses.
A maddening itch stretched beneath my skin.

You see them, mangy, streaking round the bins
in silver light, leaving constellations
of bloody tampons and fried chicken boxes,
but the vixen was beautiful that time I saw her
alone under the lamps. I clicked my tongue
like you would with a cat. *Do not be afraid.*

We're the scared ones, cheek by jowl with rats
and predators, permanently worried
by this tax on this city, wild things' claws
tapping out codes on lamp-lit pavements,
their thoughts as formless and half-mad as ours,
the streets a charnel of what we've buried.

My mother was right, it sounds like death
or its harbinger, trailing dirt and blood,
those cries a blade the night wouldn't sheath,
but still, the day I found the vixen dead
in the road, her sinews stiff as wood,
her fur sand-soft, her side a blush of red,

I wanted to gather her up. It isn't pretty,
love and what comes with it, and this city
I worshipped once is built on graft and chains,
and yes, I recognised that howl she made –
beneath our pelts, not much else remains
but pain and lust, and sometimes lust is pain

and skewers us, a figure-eight of blades
turning and flashing again and again,
but this is it, the price we have to pay –
and, honey, if you listen close enough
to those wild creatures keening in the dark,
some of it, to be honest, sounds like love.

RISING

The waitress at the hipster coffee shop
is shouldering a table on the pavement,
warped planks against her neck. We walk on.
Today, religion nags me like a fever
that swells, recedes, the pilgrim in me
itching to fight, but this is limbo still,
this must be Lent, cold grit stinging the blossoms,
our eyes sharp with unfelt tears, our stair-carpet
still coughing up pine needles. We're not ready
for spring's violence, the rock at the tomb
rolled away like a dream, the blinking saints
stripped of their purple drapes, pale fingers dabbling
in marble stoups, peeling back gleaming foil.
It has been fifteen, eighteen, twenty years.
This is the denial in me, the blind silver
under my tongue, the betrayal in me.
Forgive me, I am tired of dead men's voices,
how they will outlive mine. I can't read the news
but I still do. My head is full of pools
where clothes wash up unclaimed. The streets are lined
with puddles, nut husks, nitrous canisters,
shop signs with peeling Ashkenazi names,
white-capped imams. This is the history
I've swallowed whole, the Cable Street in me,
the rising, the rebellion in me.
At the canal, the sun doesn't quite break
through swollen clouds, but it lights them up
and Easter's here, as if we ever doubted,
the heat a benediction on our necks,
and, somewhere near, a messy clash of bells.

THE TOUR

It usually starts off at 5am,
an undistinguished ringroad of regret.

I once thought I'd extinguished all of them,
but here they are – my maiden cigarette,

that second bottle of indifferent wine,
the smiles of everyone who's ever fired me,

the eyes of the right girl in the wrong time
and the right man for someone else entirely.

Witness that essay when I worked my nuts off
but missed the point. Now notice if you will

that swelling chorus as the mixtape cuts off,
the babe who kissed me once she'd popped a pill,

that stupid thing I said at seventeen,
a shock of trains all shambling out of stations,

a nude ripped from a dentist's magazine,
the twisted comfort of no consolations.

Even my teeth, this morning still intact,
are harbouring a future's worth of rot

as dawn becomes another pointless fact
and sleep falls like forgiveness, though it's not.

KIDS

Women my age write poems about kids
as if they make them happen all the time,
new people, poems, miracles each year,
like that's just what you do if you're a woman
poet. But I've missed a trick, my work
and life are short on kids. It's a mistake

to think we all want kids, though my mistake
might be not having them. Look, I love kids,
don't get me wrong. I also love my work
and to be honest I've just not had time,
plus I'm married to another woman,
an issue (understatement of the year)

if you do want kids. In my second year
of college a kid would have been a mistake,
but now it's like I'm not a proper woman
if I don't stop mucking about and have kids,
like I'm just drinking cocktails all the time
with no sick loved ones or nightmares at work –

bitch please you don't know the meaning of work
if you don't have kids you've only got a year
or two to go you know don't you know time
is running out don't make the same mistake
so and so did left it too late for kids
missing the boat and failing as a woman –

am I even a poet, am I even a woman
if frankly this looks too much like hard work?
Why am I not a Woman Who Wants Kids
properly, what if I realise next year
that I've just made a terrible mistake
and rush for the clinic, race against time,

but pills and shots don't do the job in time
and leave me skint and scarred? I know a woman
or two that's happened to, one mistake
in bodies, blood, timing – al that work
for nothing. Maybe this will be the year
when I admit that I'm not having kids

and choose the life I know, more time to work,
to love one woman more and more each year,
escape the bittersweet mistake of kids.

MY SHADOWS

At 4am they keep me company
watching the ambulances in the street,
the first light from the Jewish bakery
spilling through the cracks like mercury,

the ones who are like me but not like me,
unlived lives branched off like arteries,
some of them wearing something like my face,
some in crinolines twisting rosaries.

Here's a male twin with my grandmother's eyes
and a spinster from the parish of Islington.
We're all good with our hands, shaking out sheets,
unknotting clouds of biro ink and cotton,

our artists' lips thinning around pins
in this room where another me might have slept,
a child's damp head tucked underneath her chin,
a chubby hand splayed blankly on her chest,

or where she might have clutched herself and wept
at the weight of all this motherhood
that wants to overwhelm her every night
and that, for me, was just another road

my headlights swept before I headed home.
Now they're here too, children never grown,
the answer that, unknown, remains unknown,
my chosen road that will not let me go.

DIVINING

Some people look for signs in silk-wrapped cards
and end-of-pier machines. We count tears, sneezes,
steps, imagined sheep, clumps of tea leaves,
as if something larger than everyday life
speaks through them, like our eyes might deceive us
if we forget. My childhood litanies
were strung like seed-small beads on rosaries,
mysteries numbered in sevens and threes.

The believers bartered their acts of contrition
with prayers hard and precise as sugared almonds.
Ten Hail Marys weighted my palms like diamonds,
my fingers ticking off the meditations
in the dark behind a purple curtain,
straining my ears to hear the painful lessons
of grown-up lives and all their unasked questions
howling behind those numbers, small and certain.

Even now, though I'm not superstitious
about ladders, black cats or pavement cracks,
one glimpse of a lone magpie takes me back
to a kind of blind faith, and I can't resist
counting – three for a girl, four for a boy,
a fragile credo, but it never fails,
a dizzy streak of silver in the rails,
that second bird – the one that stands for joy.

HONEYCHILD

For Oralia

Too small to cry, a pulsing scrap of life,
you slid into the world. They pulled the curtain
of hospital green between you and your mother
and taped you up with tubes. Your ancient gaze,

old and dark as God, took it all in. Your breath
reached for the sky, sucking it back to you
like milk-sweet skin, the white cap on your hair
proud as a tribal wrap. You were staying right here.

Me and your mum danced in the bass-drenched back
of basement clubs, teetering on plush spikes,
chugging snakebite and black. Prison-thin cigs,
stained student walls sheathed in Indian silk,

and me and your mum like temple priestesses
lazily gilding ourselves all afternoon,
listening to women singing about the pain
we used to be so hungry to embrace,

and now she's making me renounce Satan
in a town that looks like the ones we escaped
all for you, godchild, a gold gift-wrap bow
perched in your hair as a lovestruck vicar

drops an unprompted kiss on your head
and trails your starfish fingers in the water
that binds us – you and me, your mum, her man,
his brother, murmuring, *Amen, Amen,*

when the sermon hits home. I don't pray these days
but I will for you. I have more than one wish
for you, that your friends become sisters like she was
to me, that no one will ever hand you the world

like a blighted peach, showing you its good side.
I want you to know I'm there, a lighted car
on the dark roadside waiting for you
to come inside, and I am staying right here.

MILK AND HONEY

And when that morning comes
let me get up, go into the kitchen,
fire up the stove in the first shaft of sun.

Let the winter burn itself away,
the garden's veins thick with sudden life,
nubs of petals blazing in the clay.

Let me anoint my face with oil of roses,
hands and lips with henna and scarlet.
I'll wear my ink-soft market-stall robes

to knead dough, strew pomegranate seeds
like damp jewels. Saffron, ras el hanout,
mounds of spice with tiny folded buds.

I'll light the white fig candles from Paris,
polish the china and lead-crystal glasses.
Nothing will be too good, too much for us.

Now let me welcome all of you at the door,
hungry, tired, cheeks scented with frost,
cold still clinging to your coats like stars –

here's an unborn son twisting in the water
like a glistening fish under taut skin.
Here's an old lover, a grave-eyed daughter

and friends I thought I'd never see again,
my grandmothers in camel coats and pearls,
dead boys clutching lilies and champagne.

Come in, come in – you don't know how long
I've been standing watching the garden thaw,
listening for the first notes of the song

that brings me out of my numbered years,
calling me to you and whatever's there,
my arms held out, ready, without fear.

BLUES

I call you from the bar where the red sign
blisters and glows w th rain. On stage, a line
of women sing, their foreheads pearled with brine.

This blues is whisky and razor-blade gin,
do-me-wrong lines worn Bible-page thin.
I grab a glass, usher the darkness in,

alight for you. Here holiness meets noise,
hollering upward, tears in a woman's voice
threaten to break as I make the choice

I knew I would, and slip out as the whine
of brass and horns and keys yearns and combines
to walk the streets between your night and mine,

your wrought-iron rails looming like a wreck
on a dark sea, two glasses on the deck,
the bass of your hip the clef of your neck

on boiled white sheets where my fingers twine,
forging new notes in an unbroken line,
stroking the sleeping keyboard of your spine.

LIFE MODEL

Those shoulders are deceptive. She was born
to work the land, broad-beamed, her calves all brawn,
Michelangelo chest with tits sketched on.

Twelve years old, she walked through galleries
seeing her thighs on cherubs. Worried eyes
stared back from glass over gold-shot skies.

Aged seventeen, she dressed like Frida Kahlo,
hair crowned with flowers, steel backbone, dark arrow,
but still her legs were made to plough and furrow.

At twenty-five, she was full to the brim
with elbows, knees. Her heartbeat found its twin.
Stretchmarks carved creeks of light in her skin.

On her twenty-sixth birthday, a new tattoo
gave birth to another – one swallow, then two,
swooped down her back in faded sailor's blue.

At thirty, she looks around at eager faces
and drops her robe, skin starting to sing,
wide, strong shoulders growing paper wings,

crotch a dark scribble, thighs still there,
belly a lush pillow, eyes still clear,
feet planted wide, all of her finally here.

HIDE

It started small, a geometric kiss
in crimson on your wrist. rogue showers of stars
etched down your hips, a cocktail glass,
a hand of cards. We loaded up your car,

my lap bright with CDs, you at the wheel.
You christened me your good-luck charm
as blistering grey towers gave way to moors,
a girl with my hair, my dress, on the flesh of your arm.

Your armour grew, a Coney Island sprawl
of ink – a Ferris wheel, a motel sign,
pink flamingos. You decked your girl in jewels.
On the struts of your back, whole cities bloomed.

At night I map you, borders growing thin,
looking for just one inch of naked skin.

ASCENSION

Christ, we look young here. The absence of years
works on our black-and-white faces like bleach.
At the edge of the shot, out of reach
but near, there are recriminations, tears –
what the hell did we know of love's violence,
how it could tear the spine out of a night,
blight a few years? All we knew was white
pillow-notes, nonsense about figs and incense,
the spill of glitter from the card you sent
one February glinting from the cracks
in my hall floor for years, Sundays spent
glorying in our skins, the stinging lack
on Mondays. This could not be what you meant
when, later, you asked if I wanted you back –

there was no back. You can't uncrack the spine
of a book, even a loved one. When I look
at the letters, postcards, tickets I took
from our wreckage, they're heavy with signs
of wrongness, rot. But that night in Australia
I almost forgot, a church in the heart
of your mate's Sydney suburb showing the art
of my favourite artist, Bill Viola –
remember, the three of us went to see
a body spiralling up from the altar
on video screens. I grabbed your knee
as that lone figure rose through fire and water,
and now I know the wound you made in me
would one day be the point where light could enter.

A DOZEN SUNSETS

In our last week, you brought me roses,
orange bruised with red. A dozen sunsets,
you said, pleased with yourself. Then, a few days

after that, you told me about her,
and how you'd fucked each other in the bracken,
and if I cared more, I'd have seen the bruise

she left on you, that if I had been smarter
I wouldn't trust you, though you'd asked me to.
That night I hacked those roses into embers

with our knives, scratched my arms until they bled
to stave off deeper scars. But the fire
of that night spread and laid waste to five years

in a few hours. Even Paddington station,
where I once met you every Friday night,
seemed blurred to me, seen through a scrim of ash,

but if I had the ashes of that night
I'd capture them in a dark, squarish jar,
something you'd like – something artisan –

and leave them in a bar, or on a train
to Bude or Rhyl, somewhere far away
anyway, so someone else cou d worry

about them for once. I'd pick up champagne
as I walked home – and flowers, those sunset roses
I told myself for years I couldn't buy

as that old image of you and her kissing
toppled in my head like demolition
and gave me back a sudden mile of sky.

LOSS

Please don't call it loss. It wasn't gym shoes.
There was no botched coin-toss, no black box,
no verdict, just a space where something was.

When you had your eye on them the whole damn time,
always kissed her goodnight, told him yes
when he stroked your thighs, I ask you, was that loss?

If it's big enough for a polished box,
if the line drops, a pulse stops, is it loss?
Call its real name – fate, a bit less space

between you and the dark. It's not precise.
Everything ends, only forgetfulness
protects us from that, and no verbal gloss

blunts chaos. Besides, I won't confuse you
with exposition. All I'd say is this:
whatever else I did, I didn't lose you.

THE OTHER WOMAN

She wears a fleece and knows the names of trees.
She understands Bitcoin, blockchain and chess.
Her male friends never think of her that way.
The Other Woman isn't much like me.

The Other Woman gets from A to B.
She chairs committees, tweets at companies.
I send an emailed grievance privately.
The Other Woman's really not like me.

She studied at Life's University.
People don't find her threatening at parties.
She has no time for fiction, hip-hop, lipstick.
Your friends all say she suits you more than me.

Your parents tolerate her grudgingly.
You never stuffed her past in frayed bin bags
that split and spilled. She owns some property.
You'll never have to look for her in me.

You've got a ring now and a front-door key,
and me – I'm good. In fact, I'm moving closer
towards the woman I'd have been without you,
with everything you caged in me set free.

Sometimes I wonder when she'll start to doubt you.
That's one more thing she'll have to share with me.

I WILL SURVIVE

Deep in the countryside's coal-soft heart
I danced in the one pool of light for miles.
Drunk and in threadbare socks, I cast you off,

howling with the singer's road-rough voice
as we both cursed you for taking my joy
and more, how you had rifled cupboards, drawers,

left me bereft with a half-empty glass,
and though in public it was for the best,
my dance's essence, in its bones, was this –

that everything you took, I wanted back.
I was raw, gasping, yanked out of the black
thrashing waves, roaring like every mad

scorned bitch on earth, swigging, staying strong
because I had no choice, though every wrong
turn I'd ever made was in my feet, my throat, her song,

in every tear you didn't get to see,
in this hot mess we thought we'd never be,
in all the women dancing just like me.

SECOND SKIN

So if each seven years all your dead cells renew,
not an inch of my skin holds a memory of you.
And if that were true, man, I'd love that relief.
I'd be clean as sixteen. This suspense of belief
is brief, unconvincing, but an end to the grief.

The diaries, the posters, each letter, each card,
each photo could burn – it's the big stuff that's hard.
The in-jokes, the rhythms – forgetting the cost,
all I have could be easily torched, flogged or tossed
and remain just a fragment of all that we lost.

It's not just the albums, but whole bands and composers,
not those last flayed bouquets but whole species of roses,
not just your friends but my friends that I'd have to cull,
not just drowning my sorrows but out of my skull,
I'd lose languages, countries. My life would be dull.

So we're human. Our minds wander back to mistakes
like blood clings to viruses, bones recall breaks.
So I wore it that night, but I still kept the dress –
even with the regrets, and the night-sweats and stress.
Would I do it again? Jesus, yes. Fuck it. Yes.

ADULT EDUCATION

When I asked if your poem was about sex
it seemed the mismatched classroom held its breath.

After a pause, you said, *No, more like death*,
and awkwardly we moved on to the next

part-time writer. Perhaps I'd been direct,
but I didn't fancy you yet. We were young,

your name a brave flame on the tutor's tongue.
Later, the cricket scores would make me wet –

men with names like yours. You, or your text,
must have sparked something. Freud, dissecting dreams,

might stroke his beard, and though he'd be correct,
sometimes a thing's exactly as it seems –

later, wrapped in your bedsheets, I reflect
that great art only has so many themes.

SNOW

It's snowing. It's like the world's shut down.
There's not a soul around us in this soundless town.
And we're giggling like children – where is everyone?
Have they packed up and gone?
Has your neighbourhood fled?
The trains on their ice-throttled tracks have stopped going,
it takes a few flakes to put London to bed.
Everyone's bunking off work in the morning.
The schools and the shop-fronts are shrouded in white,
clouding the awnings. Just us and the moon,
a drowned white balloon in the scrim of the night.

You said it's OK if I don't want to come,
but I said, *I still do. Is that dumb?* Should I run
from the closeness between us, this threat of emotion,
this drop in the ocean? The truth is, I know
like champagne on my lips, the first kiss of the snow
is erosion before a whole landslide of rocks,
the tick of the clock between calm and implosion,
a house full of silence, ready to blow –
the two of us walking, our lives stacked behind us,
nobody desperate to find us. Snow.

And I guess you don't know that was when it began,
the closest I came to being crushed on a man,
but before I was sure it was anything more,
on the night of the snowfall I felt something thaw,
the shrapnel of ice that had lodged in my chest.
I could breathe, and the air caught my breath. I felt blessed.
For months I'd been numb, grief had nearly deranged me,
Christmas had come, and New Year had not changed me.
But you, you big gobshite, somehow you floored me.
You made it New Year just by walking towards me.

The last time it snowed, I was mucking around
with six lads by the pub who chucked snowballs at me,
and my hair was wet weeds as I writhed on the ground,

but still – here's the rub – I do wish you could see
that I've surrendered to joy, that I've remembered to play,
though we're no longer the girl and boy from that day
when I felt the ice lifting, the weight start to go,
creaking and shifting, the river below
surfacing, drifting, beginning to flow,
the two of us walking and talking and living,
the breath of ash on my lips. Snow.

THE BREAKFAST CLUB

The last frames always get me, the prom queen
pinning her diamond in the bad boy's ear.
I remember the wide field of your bed,
how you once caught my earring in your hand
and held it out, the triumph in your smile.

When you said I reminded you of high school
it was this America you meant.
I thought we might fold up the playing fields, the seas
between us, and be kids again,
and though you were the geek and me the goth

in our real lives, you cast me as the princess
and you, of course, the thug in tweed and swag.
I'm glad I didn't take that earring back.
I think about it in your bedside drawer,
with condoms, tickets, rolling in the dust.

The ending stays the same, the power chords,
the walking girl, the boy punching the air,
the sky held tight, two lives turned on a dime,
the earring glinting gently in your palm
as though perhaps you had it all this time.

IF YOU LIVED HERE,
YOU'D BE HOME BY NOW

If I put my palm to the glass, I think of
you, though I can't name the street where you
lived. We have faded into the map, there is no
here where you might be, where I might go. A year ago
you'd closed your social accounts. It would
be foolish to keep checking, but I do, your
home page frozen like that shop you liked
by Kentish Town tube, forlorn fifties gowns
now bleached blue-white, all of it long shut down.

If I put out my tongue for snow, I think of
you, though this is the hottest day of the year. You
lived whole lives before me and I envied them all.
Here is a photo of you sleeping, taken by someone
you'd loved more, longer. I could never
be that for you now. I can't reach out, can't call you
home. That line is cut, the fuses blew
by the last time I left. I might be listening but
now there's nothing, nothing, nothing at all of you.

THE BOOK OF GOODBYES

Hard to record the substance of goodbyes,
the awkward elbow-clasp as doors swing wide,
the desperate small talk of the taxi ride,

the sudden rush of what we should have said
when later, our unburied sorrow finds us
packing a bag, stripping down a bed,

instead of that lame stuff, a duff translation
of love, an awkward hand held up, a bluff
I'll call you from the platform at the station.

The car says, *You have reached your destination*,
then silence falls. Sometimes I tell myself
that somehow, somewhere, our goodbyes are stored

and bound between black spines, each offering
falling just short, invariably flawed,
the pages heavy as a broken thing.

CALL ME DOLORES

Call me Dolores. I'm your waitress today.
I know you wouldn't think you'd find me here
slinging plates in a motorway café
with my wrist-cuffs, Cons, spiked hair and ears.
Ah, well. You know what? It is what it is.
My mammy told me there'd be days like this.

Before this I was the youngest of seven
snug in the back of a donkey-slow car,
shoving my brothers, roads wide as rivers,
static radio maundering about a war
with no end or beginning, troubles as long
as death. Something fell from my mouth: song.

Call me Dolores – my mammy's idea,
that was. She loved Our Lady, the words
of the Sorrowful Mysteries kissing my ear.
I pinned my heart on like a medal from Lourdes,
wore it outside, lugging this heavy name,
seven sorrows too much for one small frame.

Then I was that girl in the year above
with plum-dyed hair and granddad shirts who smoked
on the swings, the one your boyfriend loved,
the babe with the bottle of whisky-laced Coke
whose lilting laugh cracked the gospels to bits
as pub-door posters gave way to *Smash Hits*.

Call me Dolores; it's on the rap sheet,
the rider, the prescription, the tour bus.
Six years of neon cathedrals in bare feet,
six years of hunger looking for a phone box
to call my family, swallowing the pride
caught in my breath, a stitch, a wound in my side.

One day I'll get the band back on the road.
We'll cue up playlists, vinegar on our lips
from last night's chips, coffee long gone cold,
the struts of bridges opening like ribs,
hands on the wheel mapping the fading stars,
pale wrists strung like the necks of guitars.

Call me Dolores. This is what I want:
for my head to be quiet. To stop asking why.
To get myself a new name at the font,
tilt back my head and fall out of the sky.
To feel the headlights kissing my closed eyes.
To be a road movie where nobody dies.

ANCESTRY

Sometimes when I pluck a champagne flute
from a waiter's tray at a publishing party

I think of my distant stonemason uncles
who came down from a spire on a windy day,

went to the pub and never came back,
and know how easily I could do that.

When I squat in the dirt plucking raspberries
from pale stalks I become my mother's nonna

bundled in widow's black, chasing chickens
through cold backyards. When I put on lipstick

I shrug on the silk of that snake-crazy auntie
who taught all of us not to marry for beauty,

but still, it feels right that the local hipsters
outside the barber mutter *Mamma mia*

through their beards when my hips churn past them.
All my relatives are called Paul and Maria

on my mother's side, like a Scorsese wedding.
My dad's lot are different. Something in us

is drawn to stone, adept at building walls,
and when I walk through this raging city

past a woman with one leg and no face
I think about my father's father's mother,

who took no money for the cards she read
and when she died the church was full of strangers,

and what I have of hers – a sequined bag
the shape of a pig's heart, a chip of blood

in a gilt ring, a foreignness, a knack
for gut feelings, reading the twitch of an eye,

and I know her, another dark woman, alone
in a field full of stones, trying to die.

JUKEBOX

I coveted my big cousin's jukebox
that her sister has now in her front room,
the lyrics cradled in its neon tubes
keeping something of her safe at home.

The cardboard click and flap as the tracks drop
brings back sluggish summer afternoons,
one-hit wonders dropping in our laps
by pool tables in seaside pub back rooms,

a scrunchie round her wrist, the disco ball
that starred the walls of her twenty-first,
and the music for her funeral –
when things are bad, they can still get worse.

Songs, getting older, waiting behind glass
for the girl who, on her wedding day,
took off her shoes and ran across the grass.
God knows how you choose what song to play

for someone who'd so recently worn white
to take the floor – it all cut off too soon,
a couple turning underneath the light,
a chaplain playing 'Fly Me to the Moon'.

A GEORDIE GRANDMA FORESEES
HER DEATH

Eeh, ah'm not worried, pet. When it's me time
to gan ah'll gan sur divven't fret, nee bother.
Ah've browt up fawa bairns from different fathas,
and wor Michelle's an aal. Everyone in toon
knaas me name, like, but they just caal us Nana.
When ah think aboot death, ah see some auld gadgie
wi nee teeth in his gob, aal red and radgie.
It might be like a nap, that'd be canny,
ah'd not mind that. Aye, there's always pills
if it gets bad, a few glasses o' wine
and that's that. Yer a bonry lass, it's fine,
ah've had me prime, seen friends and bairns get ill
an' that. Ah'm paggered, pet, ah've had me fill
an' it was cushty. Haway, Death – yer mine.

LATIN

Caecilius est in horto. Nothing new;
Pompeii's been burning since we first got boobs,
its lovers cast in chalk. We watch the clock,
our navy skirts rolled over at the top.

I think I love Claire, her noblewoman's ringlets.
I'd stand on the rock of Masada for her,
brave-faced in death. She's a senior prefect,
straight As, second soprano like me

but more perfect. I try to touch her hair,
chicken out quickly, laugh and kick her chair.
Odi et amo, don't ask me how.
Vivamus, mea Lesbia. She glares.

Nobody likes Quintus. Sara Whitecroft
smokes round the back of the science block.
Bex has stopped eating. *Cerberus est in via.*
Mina's dad hasn't been home in weeks.

This is a good school; it will not fail us.
We are good girls; we think this will suffice.
Perhaps we'll get more beautiful than this,
but what we won't have is this innocence,

our breath blameless as milk. It's all to come,
the sex, Silk Cut and snakebite of sixth form.
We stand up as the bell goes. *Valedixit:*
the hot engulfing of an ordered city.

THE GIRL ON THE WALL AT COSTA

I want to be the girl on the wall at Costa
with her milky skin and dark feathered fringe,
her tucked-in smile under a red umbrella
that lights her like a lamp. I know it's strange

but I want to be the girl on the wall at Costa,
that chunky scarf, her jacket soft black leather,
just hanging there ignoring the barista
pouring foamed milk, inscribing a dark feather

or fern or star onto soft caps of white
for long-haul truckers and sweat-stale commuters,
young grass-stained mums, writers on all-nighters,
white lipsticked lids grimacing by computers.

As I stand before work in the Bowie muzak
I wish I was that girl with the red umbrella
who could be off to record some music
or see a man about her new novella –

and yes, I know she's a stock-photo poster
and may not even know she's on this wall,
but I want to be the girl on the wall at Costa,
smiling and smiling, like she has it all.

CONVERSATIONAL ITALIAN

My family mangled it so it wasn't a language
so much as an argot, an attitude, a hug,
the feel of an uncle's cigar-scented fingers
pinching my cheek. First, you learn to shrug,
smack lips on curses – that guy is a sperm,
that girl's pussy is a wooden fig.

Don't reheat minestrone or return
to last night's soup or a lukewarm affair.
'Course I'm not English, look at this hair,
but I can't read Dante and turn red when waiters
offer *grazie* and watch my lips for *prego*
like wartime. *Where you from, though?* Here and there,

I'm leftovers, a tourist in these bones,
but my hands, look – the fluid way they move,
they've known this tide, this rhythm since the womb,
confident, smooth, punching focaccia dough,
stretching fluently, the fat heel
of my palm lathered in flour and olive oil,

and when that one Italian art editor
at work spoke to me purely in gesture
my fingers answered back. I understood
the language was in me all along
and what I am has settled in my hands,
moving and speaking my real mother tongue.

DIARY, 1999

Talcum powder – good on greasy hair
but not too much! Meet M at Central Station
24-hour café. Chamber Choir.
Dutch Revolt. Draft Counter-Reformation.

See M in Courtyard. Prizegiving Rehearsal.
Top Shop. Yates's Wine Lodge. Wife of Bath.
Bring tinned goods for Harvest Festival.
Angela Carter. John Paul Sartre. Plath.

To what extent does this theory apply?
Think I love M. Write essay about schism.
Gained two pounds. Managed not to cry,
there's always purging. Presbyterianism.

M and I Did It. Practice flicky eyes.
What were the French Wars of Religion about?
Comedies of this time include disguise.
Got high. Watched *Magic Roundabout*.

Ottoman Decline. Prep for debate.
Song for end of term with Mr Craggs.
Reverse Parking. Protest Clause 28.
Try not to look too gay though. Two more shags.

First fight with M. I told her I'd skipped lunch.
Discuss the workings of the Privy Council.
Made up again. Buy stamps, four-hole punch,
Cajun lipstick. General Interest: Cancelled.

Record *Sopranos*. Nacho recipe.
How accurate is this interpretation?
Treaty of Yam Zapolsky. Got a B.
Revise the bloody Counter-Reformation.

Now 44. Tequila. Macy Gray.
Feel free to back this up with your own knowledge.
Why does September seem so far away?
Said goodbye to M. Can't wait for college.

CHOKED

A week after it happened, I choked
on stage for the first time, my tongue

artless and thick. It's still like digging rocks
up with my teeth, saying what he'd done.

The police tried. I've got the paper still
that they filled out, but all the words I knew

drifted away from me as my nights shortened
and my solitude grew doors and corners.

In two weeks I was back on stage headlining
but though the words came back, they weren't enough

to block it out. Nothing was – self-defence, crying,
locking the door he pushed me up against,

smiling, lying. Nothing drowned the sound
that fell from me that night, trying to shout

and all that came out was the sound of words dying.

TALKING TO WOMEN

For God's sake, guys, listen. Stop talking to women
in that irreverent way you still think is so damn shocking to
women.

Don't worry, we won't faint at your complex arguments.
Do you not think that how you speak sounds mocking to
women?

Panels of pale suits on daytime television
are explaining abortion, domestic violence and stalking to
women.

Such mysterious creatures, ponder nice-guy romantics,
presumably seizing a dozen red roses and flocking to women.

But what do they really want? wonder agency creatives,
over moodboards of whatever new crap they're hawking to
women.

What if they can no longer sell pink biros and razors,
feminine sprays and new brands of silk stocking to women?

God give me wisdom, give me strength to shape a world
of gentle men, of growth, of doors unlocking to women.

SPARROW

For Pamela Sue Anderson

This woman, dark-robed, fine-boned, light as a
sparrow thrown by a possible god,
flies through tangled streets, arched corridors,
swiftly swoops through circumstance and gowns
in through the doorway thick with noise and light,
through the blazing hall, smiling at each
one of us in turn as the ancient
door slams shut. Thinking of her reminds me
of the parable, Bede's bird hurled through
the rafters of the rowdy, roaring, bright
hall where warriors raised their studded cups
and, in a heartbeat, the bird flying back
out past the nodding trees into the night,
through what exists, what doesn't, and what might –
another bird, another source of light.

THE POND BRIDE

Still open-eyed, I plunge into the pond,
past the smack of cold through the shock,
and force the dregs of London into my blood,
carrion, syringes, bad medicine,
stained tins, burnt wicks. I gulp the cold tea
and old cabbage of the city's guts.

I'm a bride making my way through the chambers,
sparkling columns looming out of the dark,
head a coronet of drowning stars,
feet netted with pearls, plummeting in a comet
of spilled mercury, my wedding train
fine and white and plentiful as smoke.

My blood knows its elements, the ink,
moss and stone; an untethered veil
of hair wraps my bleached face. The trapped echoes
of a lost world put the city on mute,
block out my life on the other side,
the shouts from the far banks, the artless light,

my friends calling. When I climb back out
the air is pale silk, not dense velvet.
My limbs are heavy with the water's weight.
She knows me, she's claimed me. The chill in my bones
won't quite let go. Somewhere in the dark
under the streets, my other bride is waiting.

BAKING FOR ANGELS

Angels are chilling in my kitchen again.
Bread-baking days I set my watch by them,
clattering down, filling the air like sleet,
drizzling feathers on my baking sheets.
Early on, it started small, a thin
feathered flash at the edge of my vision,
growing until the windows flushed with wings,
heaven-red eyes, heavy, polished limbs.
I don't ask why they're here, why they came,
just watch them fold their wings in the doorframe,
knocking their tips, more feathers than you'd think
like rippling fabric arching up and in,
muscle and bone a flexing, twisting coat.
Now I've stopped drinking more of them come to eat,
open-mouthed, waiting. Under my bare toes
piles of feathers swirl like dry snow,
quite ordinary, really. No, I don't
read the Psalms, but songs come from their throats,
sounding like cymbals in another room
tumbling slowly down, and that sound blooms
until your ears are full. Their skin glows
vellum-yellow and taut, but it's those
wings I love, how they slap softly like a
Xerox machine spewing great sheets of white –
you'll see it once they finish up and fly,
zigzagging back across the gaping sky.

HYMN

I believe in the hanging plum-glazed ducks
of Gerrard Street, in the neon song
of sex and phone boxes, all the bad luck
waiting upstairs, and the falling gauze
of a smoke-blue Soho evening.

I believe in chicken shops and drums
of fruit and saltfish. Jehovah's phone shops,
the clashing tongues of all-night vigils,
headwrapped goddesses, weaves in the gutters,
spoils of war and raised scars of loss.

We have come down from the hills and suburbs
clutching our battered copies of *The Face*,
forsaking our parents' four-bedrooms, clean air,
the sea's sweet mouth, friends from our youth,
green squares. So ruin me, London, I dare you,

grope me, grab me, prop me at a bar,
I'll let you know when I've had enough,
so fuck me, London. I have chosen a god
who picked my pockets, whose touch stirred
me to joy, opened me, left me raw

for the gold-paved glint, the gospel of more,
so ghost me, London, don't call me back,
see if I care. Show me your shabby tricks,
your glass houses, your three-card blag.
Tell me your tales, I'll swallow them all.

NORTH LONDON

It's morning. All North London streams with cars,
distant neons twitching over Barnet.
The lift hums in its cage. The hall smells of cigars.

White headlights are like spotlights. It's still half-dark.
Two Caribbean women talk, their voices ascending,
a shock of green-tailed birds.

Here are mock-Tudor copies of Park Crescent.
Frail pre-Raphaelite schoolgirls brandishing smartphones.
The heavy walk of disappointed women.

This new Italian restaurant has an app.
Some trophies wait for names.
I watch a man stacking plums
gently as eggs, each fruit a bruised sun.

By the noticeboard with its lost-looking palms,
thin girls are modelling leopard-print scarves.
A couple cross the road in a helix of arms.

A dominatrix waiting for the bus
watches a diva with a Mulberry bag spark a first fag.
Kids' scooters are carried home by abashed dads.

Today's headlines say, *After the Verdict, More Rage.*
The sky looks half-erased and oddly static.
They say we're due another spate of winter.

Trees twenty times taller than me are swaying.
Their gentle movement looks somehow amused,
like they're whispering, *Look up once in a while.*

EDINBURGH

A sea of whispers from the Mile to Leith –
How are your buckets? A squall of drums
drowns out the answer as the city's patience
frays and restores itself again. Rain comes

and agents don't. The Fringe has made us pilgrims,
begging, consoling. *No, it's not us, mate,
it's the tourists, Tuesday's always like this.*
A drunk bends his inked neck to the rain's blades.

It's all about the coins, their heat, their smell
of blood and fingers, dank long-suffering bars
with tills awash in middle-class kids' shrapnel,
firework storms embarrassing the stars

as we trudge back up constant hills and stairs
that promise us the moon. We leave the banks
slumbering undisturbed like winter bears,
our pockets full of euros and Swiss francs.

THURSDAY NIGHT IN THE
BROKEN HEARTS HOTEL

No soft places, no shade. A lone orchid
throttled by pebbles in a test-tube.
The wet-room cupboard leaks towards the bed.

Last night's bloodstain, a tired accident,
soaped from red to ochre just after dawn,
waits half-hidden for the chambermaid.

The coffee machine with its gunmetal pods
could outwit Steve Jobs. Down in the bar
they're serving Italian-Japanese fusion

with menus thicker than Gideons' Bibles.
We bring creased jackets to ruin the angles,
small sugary wine bottles in the bins.

All of it proves how easily replaced
we are. Tomorrow, someone else's face
will float on this dark window. Other feet

will flex and twitch under unsullied sheets,
the streets of this old city unimpressed,
the same river outside holding its breath.

SPACE EXPLORATION

Under this crust, there may be signs of life
pulsing on our screens like strings of gold
looped beneath planes at night. We just don't know.

There may be small boys listening to other worlds
like the one in the back of the TV,
its red-gold lodes, its smell of burning wire.

There may be stages with white-suited dancers
twirling weightlessly. There may be deserts
turning away their faces like tired women.

We do not ask. Our maps are not exact;
this end is not in sight. There may be lizards
lounging on rocks. There may be sleepy lovers

space-walking down dark halls to blazing doors;
we're just not sure. What we know is this:
that stones and gods resist. We hear them whisper,

Do not translate me. Do not get me wrong.
Please don't name me after a dead white man.
Leave me where I am. Do not kick up my dust.

THE RECORDS

I clock the doctor's adjective straight off.
Delightful, charming, meaning 'nice enough' –
challenging means 'stone mad'. That bit's a laugh,
sort of. Outside that sentence, they can't judge.

Sometimes I see their feelings limping through.
I fear suggests a card marked from the start.
A red scrawl on a file: *Such sad, sad news,*
RIP Sam, displays a blaze of heart.

All human life's here – my pretentious flatmate
who steals my pasta moaning about bunions
ruining her career, my landlord's daughter,
a nun, a convict, all these numbered someones.

You're not supposed to, but I've got my favourites.
Whiplash Man, obsessed with litigation,
the pastels of the Make-a-Wish Foundation,
some mum's worst nightmare cobbled into data,

and under it there's so much left unsaid,
a breeze stirring the nets, a torn-off sob,
a muttered pledge – knock the fags on the head.
Wear better shoes. Get out of this job.

REVIVAL

In the first slippery hours of Sunday morning
we're partying beneath City pavements,
speaking in tongues, hands in the air, redeemed.

They never told you God was portable
but here He is, shaking the foundations,
temple gates vanishing in the rubble.

No saint or prophet would call this a vigil
but it's still religion. A neon-haloed angel
blesses the decks, heart on her vest

bleeding serene trails between her breasts.
She raises a chalice. Worshippers dance
in a mass of guilt and dry-ice incense.

We're the wise ones – cracked parables, lost days,
chemical visions, nights without bridegrooms,
faces raised to the wild light. Reverence. Praise.

THE THAW

We met in January. London was thawing,
the city shaking out their stiffened nets.
My old flat, I saw swathes of town from there,
five different sets of fireworks for New Year.
I fixed my face, the sky steadily warming.

The night before, I'd staggered on the ice,
my weight unspooling like a coil of rope,
and fallen a few minutes from the house.
Seeing you was like that, a twist of hope
making me weightless, lost. Behind the glass

you raised your head and smiled. The ritual
first-date dance began, then the whisper
of something bigger – *this is going well* –
made itself known, and like the night before
I thought, *I'm going to fall, so I will fall.*

This was no spring, but still it was the thaw
of everything, a shift towards the light.
The lamps came on and bleached the wet roads white.
As chairs stacked up around us in the night,
we fell together through an open door.

MARRIAGE SONG

In blue silk knickers I attempt the gown.
My maid of honour zips me at the back.
The tattooed stylist tries my hair up, down.
Mum fastens Nana's pearls around my neck.

In the next room the starters shine like mirrors
in clingfilm. I hear they've brought the flowers.
We strike a pose in front of borrowed windows,
the flash pops, and the rain we've had for hours

suddenly stops. This is what's happening,
a bar or two of chatter from the stairs,
busboys outside sweeping up cigarettes,
commuters' lips that might be mouthing prayers

or curses behind glass. Sounds go astray,
the stairwell like a diving bell, wet roads
on fire with light. We're short on things to say.
My father loops my arm in his. You're there,

suddenly, somewhere – I hear your steps,
your laughter. A white bed three streets away
is freshly made, sheets held like a breath.
The music starts. I think this sun might stay.

BLESSING

For Helen and Mark

Whatever is around us, we are still
restless, unsure, not trusting ourselves.
Be gentle, take a moment, take this in.
Let's declare today a holiday.
Restless, unsure, not trusting ourselves
still, we are witnessing love.
Let's declare today a holiday.
Let's politely ask the world to stop
still, we are witnessing love
in its ordinary way, in the work of a moment.
Let's politely ask the world to stop,
hold out our hands for it and wait.
In its ordinary way, in the work of a moment,
life crashes by but stops on the way back.
Hold out our hands for it and wait,
still as the stars at night.
Life crashes by but stops on the way back.
Sometimes it's easy to miss the little things.
Still, as the stars at night
tell us, what we do will always last.
Sometimes it's easy to miss the little things.
Let the way they look when they turn to each other
tell us what we do will always last.
Tell them they can rely on your goodwill.
Let the way they look when they turn to each other
be gentle. Take a moment. Take this in.
Tell them they can rely on your goodwill.
Whatever is around us, we are still.

YOUR PERSON, YOUR PLACE

Talking to married friends, I'm often struck
by their dissatisfaction over drinks,
the way they speak of closed-off avenues –

the punk rock band, the unused PhD,
the countries they can't see with her in tow,
slow concessions whittled into fractions,

oddly exact. Some still crave the exotic,
a bit of Turkish, Dutch or Shanghainese
shown off to mates like a Miami mansion.

The truth is, everyone is an adventure,
each day, each hour a possible expansion.
Every exchange of knowledge is erotic.

I like watching couples, their weird actions –
the way she loops her arms around his shoulders
like every background's a tourist attraction,

how she knows which shirt he should have worn
(not the soup-stained one) and how his head
turns to hers, a second's flare of passion –

I like to see these things, and have no answer
for the suit-wearing poet whose suspicion
of love just left frustration and inaction.

Some see it as a long-drawn-out transaction,
a war of attrition, but all I know is this:
marrying her was nothing like subtraction.

PAPER

For Heleana

After our first year, we gave each other paper
gifts to mark it, but we've been together
five years, married for one. So which date
wins and dictates the substance of the gift?
Wood, paper, leather, tin? The other day
I was chatting with an old friend from back home,

laughing at the thought of filling a home
with arbitrary gifts, not pearl and paper
but twigs, lard and Perspex. Back in the day
when my ex and I were still together,
that girl could pack rebukes into a gift –
undersized knickers, cookbooks, a date

ending in tears. After her, I didn't date
for at least a year, learned to be at home
with myself once more, embracing the gift
of solitude, admitting that on paper
she and I always looked quite good together
but we knew it might end like this one day.

Three years on I still recall the day,
the Friday lunchtime before our first date –
me and the girls eating Chinese together,
the fortune cookie's message I took home,
a promise on a piece of greasy paper,
Good thing is coming to you. A small gift,

but coming when it did, it was a gift
big enough to remember on the day
we sat down in white gowns and signed the paper,
your hand on mine, your maiden name, the date,
the raft of presents in the taxi home,
an envelope sealing our lives together.

Now we dance in the kitchen to 'Let's Stay Together'
on *Steve Wright's Sunday Love Songs*. The gift
is your deep sleep-breath, the bones of the home
we're building. So, my love. who cares what day
it is, what year? Regardless of the date
or what we've chosen to wrap up in paper,

for us to be together every day
is the real gift – Sunday, after a date,
the two of us at home reading the paper.

MORTGAGE

Derived from a Law French term meaning 'death pledge'

The Nest, you called it on your spreadsheets, meaning the
house, the foundations you craved. You said to me, *It
feels like I can't live without it.* So I lived with your need,
its edges crowding our rented flat. I knew it had to be our
own or nothing. But houses have secrets, maybe a
constellation of woodworm in the beams, shadow tricks
of a history surveyors may not spot. I fretted about the
nails, the plaster, the boiler. You anchored us with paper,
holding reams of letters in drawers I painted green,
the garden stirring under half-dead leaves. Our four new
walls held us. We put down roots, starting with our breath
together, end of the line, for better, for worse, till death.

BLOEMENMARKT

Easy enough to leave a hotel room
on a blue morning, the air crushed diamonds,
a slanted note propped on the sheets – *Back Soon.*

Easy to be in love in Amsterdam
in trainers and fake fur. The doorman's wink
gives a quick nod to everything I am

while last night's flat champagne chills in the sink.
Easy to stride across Museum Square
for ten-euro roses, red laced with ink

in plastic pails. You'd think love would be harder
on a damp Tuesday Megabus to Bristol,
in two narrow beds at an airport hotel,

or at a funeral two days before Christmas –
but those days never made me any less
grateful for you, or any less in love.

Here I am in my thirties, someone's wife,
mad hair, no makeup, rushing towards midlife,
bearing dripping flowers, nothing to prove.

SOLSTICE

For lovers, every day's the shortest day,
but when we wake and see the winter's laid
its frost-bleached light across our shimmering bed
I reach for your elbow and ask you to stay
right where you are. We'll watch the garden glow,
one sugared apple in a hat of snow.

Our tree preens like a wise man in the kitchen.
Today we'll leave a cardboard door ajar
on something good, an angel or a star.
Gold candle-ends are guttering and twitching
but this dried-out year, dawdling to a close,
makes a dead sunflower-head a Christmas rose.
Let's not snip ribbon-ends or burnish pastries,
tick off lists, chase the tails of our lives.
We know other ways to be good wives,
this whole slovenly day ours for the tasting.
When the world's stopped clock beckons us to love,
may God grant us the wisdom not to move.

Put on the CD from a long-dead friend,
the carols twisting silver filaments
of holly crowns and slaughtered innocents.
This is the time for watching things end.
A frozen heel of bread, two stunted eggs,
the coffee pot spits out the year's dark dregs,
gather them up, bring them back to bed.
Let's have it all now, brilliantly clear,
the miracle of what's already here.
Let's let the words stay on our tongues unsaid.
The world will be back with us soon enough,
the year's deep night, and the morning of us.

NOTES

'Ascension': refers to video artist Bill Viola's *Tristan's Ascension*, displayed in Redfern, Australia, in 2008.

'The wound is the place where the light enters you' – Rumi

'The Other Woman': inspired by two poems, Roddy Lumsden's 'The Man I Could Have Been' and American poet Cheryl B's poem on a similar theme.

'A Geordie Grandma Foresees Her Death': while the title is taken from Yeats' Irish Airman, this is a (very loose) version of John Donne's 'Death Be Not Proud.' *Gadgie*: bloke, man (from the Romany), *radgie*: angry, *paggered*: exhausted; *cushty*: lovely.

'Latin': includes familiar phrases and characters from the Cambridge Latin Course.

'Talking to Women': one translation of the word ghazal – this poem's form – is 'talking to women', so I thought it would be a good form for a poem about mansplaining.

'Sparrow': uses the line from St Bede, 'This sparrow flies swiftly in through one door of the hall, and out through another.'

'Your Person, Your Place': title from Philip Larkin's poem 'Places, Loved Ones'.

'Mortgage': a reverse 'golden shovel', using a line from Tomas Transtromer's 'A Winter Night': 'The house feels its own constellation of nails/holding the walls together.'

'Bloemenmarkt': the floating flower market in Amsterdam.

'Solstice': inspired by John Donne's 'A Nocturnal upon St Lucie's Day' and another poem related to Donne's, Jo Bell's brilliantly bawdy 'Things Which Are'.

ACKNOWLEDGEMENTS

My thanks first of all to Clive Birnie and Bridget Hart of Burning Eye Books, and to Harriet Evans for her sensitive copy-editing.

Acknowledgements are due to the editors of the following publications, in which some of these poems first appeared under different titles: *Visual Verse*, *The Beacon* and *The Very Best of 52: A poem for every week of the year* (Nine Arches Press, 2015).

Thanks to Roman Krznaric, Steve Larkin, Paul Burston, Bobby Nayyar and Alan Buckley for their encouragement over the years, and Will Holloway for his editing of the final draft. Thanks to my tutors, Roddy Lumsden, Kate Potts, Annie Freud and Katy Evans-Bush, and to Krystyna FitzGerald-Morris for the cover image.

Love to Polari, the Persisters and the Goats.

Thank you to my parents Christina and David, and to Aimee, Ella, Helen, Kerry-Anne and Nancy. Welcome to the world, Oralia and Evita.

Finally, thank you to my cover girl, Mrs Heleana Blackwell, for everything.